IT'S TIME TO EAT ONIONS

It's Time to Eat ONIONS

Walter the Educator

Silent King Books
A WhichHead Entertainment Imprint

Copyright © 2024 by Walter the Educator

All rights reserved. No part of this book may be reproduced in any manner whatsoever without written per- mission except in the case of brief quotations embodied in critical articles and reviews.

First Printing, 2024

Disclaimer

This book is a literary work; the story is not about specific persons, locations, situations, and/or circumstances unless mentioned in a historical context. Any resemblance to real persons, locations, situations, and/or circumstances is coincidental. This book is for entertainment and informational purposes only. The author and publisher offer this information without warranties expressed or implied. No matter the grounds, neither the author nor the publisher will be accountable for any losses, injuries, or other damages caused by the reader's use of this book. The use of this book acknowledges an understanding and acceptance of this disclaimer.

It's Time to Eat ONIONS is a collectible early learning book by Walter the Educator suitable for all ages belonging to Walter the Educator's Time to Eat Book Series. Collect more books at WaltertheEducator.com

USE THE EXTRA SPACE TO TAKE NOTES AND DOCUMENT YOUR MEMORIES

ONIONS

It's time to eat onions, round and so bright,

It's Time to Eat
Onions

With layers inside, hidden from sight.

They come in all colors—white, red, and gold,

Adding bold flavor, both young and old.

In salads, they're crunchy, sliced thin and sweet,

Adding a zip that can't be beat.

With every crisp bite, they give a surprise,

A tangy delight for our taste and our eyes.

In soups, they're so cozy, soft as can be,

Melting in broth like leaves on a tree.

Cooked nice and gentle, they bring out the best,

Making each spoonful warm and blessed.

Sautéed in a pan, they sizzle and brown,

Softening up, turning golden all 'round.

Their smell fills the kitchen, warm and so sweet,

Making each bite a special treat.

It's Time to Eat
Onions

On sandwiches too, they add a nice crunch,

Perfect in salads, dinners, or lunch.

With lettuce and cheese, they're happy to blend,

Onions bring flavor from end to end.

Some onions are tiny, like pearls in a jar,

But their taste is mighty, no matter how small they are.

They twinkle in dishes, like stars from above,

Adding a burst of flavor we love.

In pasta or stew, they shine in each bite,

Turning the meal tasty and bright.

Whether raw, cooked, or roasted to brown,

Onions bring smiles, never a frown.

Sometimes they're tangy, and sometimes they're sweet,

A mix of both makes them a treat.

Layer by layer, they hide their fun,

It's Time to Eat
Onions

A rainbow of taste for everyone.

They grow underground, with roots that hold tight,

Waiting to reach for the warm sunlight.

Once pulled from the earth, they're ready to share,

A kitchen surprise beyond compare.

It's Time to Eat
Onions

So next time you see one, give onions a cheer,

For adding bold flavor, day after year.

ABOUT THE CREATOR

Walter the Educator is one of the pseudonyms for Walter Anderson. Formally educated in Chemistry, Business, and Education, he is an educator, an author, a diverse entrepreneur, and he is the son of a disabled war veteran. "Walter the Educator" shares his time between educating and creating. He holds interests and owns several creative projects that entertain, enlighten, enhance, and educate, hoping to inspire and motivate you. Follow, find new works, and stay up to date with Walter the Educator™

at WaltertheEducator.com

www.ingramcontent.com/pod-product-compliance
Lightning Source LLC
LaVergne TN
LVHW051922060526
838201LV00060B/4125